ISBN (978-1482527308)

Foreword

My human was kind enough to write this story for me as I have a hard time typing. We discussed this story everyday as I relayed my experiences in the Corporate World.

For my first job, I really did not know what to expect but with determination and persistence, I was able to communicate my experiences and wanted to share them with other corporate employees.

CONTENTS

Introduction

This is a tongue - in- cheek short story illuminating some of the obvious and literal language used by corporations today. It is a story that will hopefully evoke humor and reflection. So, take a break, find your humor, and enjoy.

I asked myself, what would a dog think? Hopefully, some of you will nod your head, laugh and say "Oh, yes."

Did you know that the cubicle workspace was created in 1967? That was over 40 years ago! According **to Cooper Schmidt,** *a Corporate Employee new to the workplace, he sees this as a sort of kennel and wonders why humans actually like this or do they...*

Chapter 1
"The Best Day Ever"

I could not believe it! I finally got my first new job and it was for everyday! I would be getting up every morning and going to work just like a human! My name is **Cooper Schmidt** and I am a Corporate Dog.

It all began when my human came home and was telling me about an open position for a delivery person at a company that hired all kinds of employees.

"Do you think I could apply?" I asked. "I have been to school and have learned so many things! I know all about grooming, chasing, catching, and I can sit and stay when asked to. Oh please let me apply."

My human sat there awhile, drank her coffee, and looked like she was considering my plea. Then she said, "Sure, you can apply." "Let's get your papers in order, license, vaccinations, immunizations and so forth and we can go down to the resource department tomorrow morning."

That was great news for me! I dusted off my tweed vest that I keep for special times. *At my school, my instructor always said to look your best and to look professional.*

The next morning we headed off to the resource department where I applied for my first job. It was a long piece of paper that asked a lot questions about my education, my personality and what breed I was. The form went on to ask if I was ever bad or ever been up to any mischief. I did not know exactly what that meant, so I answered "no".

I continued to fill out the form with speed and efficiency. The human at the office was very nice and graciously shook my paw and said, "We will be in touch." *I was not sure what "being in touch" actually meant but nodded my head in agreement.*

Later that day, I received a call from the company. The resource department called me to come in for an interview for the position of the corporate delivery employee. It was a dream come true! I jumped and rolled around on the floor with such excitement. I ran over to my human to let her know the good news. Immediately, my human said, "Let's have a quick bath and I can brush you until you shine!" I wagged my tail in anticipation of finally getting the chance to have a real job.

All night long, I sat on my bed with my favorite toy and thought about what I was going to do and say on my interview the next day. I could hardly sleep.

It was a long night, tossing and turning trying not to mess up my fur. My nails were clipped, hair brushed and a brand new collar awaited me. I also sported my tweed vest that matched my coloring. I looked great. My collar was brown leather and had a shiny blue tag on it with my name, address, and phone number. My ears were clean, teeth brushed and I was ready to go.

My human dropped me off at the front door where I was to meet Mr. Bosco. Mr. Bosco was the general manager for the company. I wondered what breed he was and if he was going to like me. As I waited in the lobby, the elevator finally lit up and out pranced Mr. Bosco. He looked like a proud German Shepard with all the right markings.  He had a slight limp in his walk but appeared very friendly.

He invited me to walk with him over to the cafeteria where we had a quiet place to discuss the job requirements and to review the company *"vision." I thought it odd as he explained that I would need to fit into a "vision," especially since I was very nearsighted but I nodded my head in agreement.* Mr. Bosco said that the company is very busy and needed someone who was enthusiastic and energetic and that this position would entail meeting and helping all the other corporate employees. He said that the delivery person was very important and much needed in the company. Mr. Bosco also told me that they were looking for someone who was independent and a *"self-starter."*

I pondered over "self-starter" because I usually start by myself, especially when I am home during the day. I start running every morning, chasing balls or squirrels. I never needed a push or shove to start running. And I always did it myself. Was that what he meant?

Mr. Bosco also told me that I would need to be able to get along with all the other corporate dogs. I told him that I was well socialized and always get along with others. *I wondered why anyone would not get along with other employees. I will have to ask my human about that as well.*

After about an hour into the interview, the decision was made. I would be hired and would start the next morning. I was so delighted to be hired for my first job and wagged my tail with great pride. I could not wait to go home with my human and let her know that I was hired for my very first job!

Chapter 2
"First Day of Work"

Dawn came and I was up with the sun. I had to go and wake up my human, as humans do like their sleep! My human made the coffee, moved around a bit as humans do in the morning then picked up my brush and straightened out my coat for my first day on the job. My human checked my ears and teeth to make sure they were clean. I could only imagine the amount of treats and biscuits I would be able to buy with all the money I was going to make. *I am not sure of why money is so important to humans but if it makes them happy it might make me happy too.*

My human drove me to my new job at around seven am and with a "Good boy" and a pat on the head, I walked through the double doors to start my day.

I said to the receptionist, "Good morning, I am Cooper Schmidt, your new corporate delivery dog." She graciously led me to the elevator and punched the fourth floor. I was a little afraid of the elevator but managed to hold my breath and not pant too much during the ride. The doors opened and I could hear the rumblings and barks of all the other corporate employees. What a great sound! It was so exciting to be with all the other corporate dogs.

I started walking down the hall to find my new boss's office. As I was walking down the hall, I glanced over the walls to see who else was working here. I had to jump up a bit to see over the walls. *Maybe they needed to be secluded from the other employees? I am not sure why everyone was behind walls but I guess I would figure that out later.* I wanted to know what they looked like, smelled like and of course, what breed they were. To my amazement, it was quite an assortment of breeds and species. I even spotted a cat and a bird! I could not believe that there were cats and birds here but I guess that is all to do with what my human calls, "*diversity*". It was certainly a diverse group of breeds and species.

I finally got to my boss's office and scratched on the door. The door read "Mr. Horatio Bosco, B.B.S." Now, I knew that B.B.S. meant Bachelor of Better Sniffing, since I learned about titles in my school. I thought to myself, "*He must be smart.*" *One day I hope I will have my B.B.S. I consider myself a really good sniffer.* He asked me to come in and sit down.

I was very nervous but happy and tried not to pant or scratch while sitting in front on my new boss. *My human said it was not appropriate to scratch or pant in front of anyone so I abided her words to a tee.* Mr. Bosco explained what I was supposed to be doing all day. He then handed me various forms to stamp with my paw and said he would give me copies later on in the day. Mr. Bosco also reviewed the dress code of the company indicating that no outrageous fur-do's or jewelry to be worn while at the company. I was comfortable with that, as I never wanted any goop in my fur and never wore any jewelry other than my collar.

Mr. Bosco explained that I have two breaks and a lunch during the day. He even said that the company has a corporate park for playtime right outside. He said that the Corporate Director of Parks and

Recreation was headed up by Ms. Pixie Browner. Mr. Bosco also said, "Ms. Pixie makes sure that everyone has a good time in the park during their breaks." Mr. Bosco also said that the corporate employees were encouraged to socialize and get to know one another. I was all for that! Mr. Bosco explained that I could have a few days off during the year for a vacation, which for me meant lying around on my favorite dog bed for the day. He also told me that if I had fleas or worms, I would need to stay home until they were gone. This made sense because the fleas like to jump around from employee to employee.

Mr. Bosco, my new corporate boss, arranged for me to attend an orientation day and to have a health checkup. The corporate health employee always wanted to make sure that no one was bringing in any dangerous worms or diseases. *Well, I hope not, I said to myself. I sure don't want to catch anything that would make me feel bad.* Mr. Bosco made the appointment with the corporate health vet for the next day. So, off we went for a tour of the company.

My new boss, simply referred to as "Bosco," escorted me down the hall to meet all the other corporate employees. As we left his office, I straightened out my collar making sure my nametag was visible. I was so proud! We turned the corner from his office and made our way from what Mr. Bosco called "the cubes." It reminded me of a kennel that I was in years ago. *I wondered how the corporate employees liked being in a cube every day. It would be like putting yourself inside a kennel voluntarily and every day*! I never liked being in the kennel and wondered if the cube would be better than a kennel. *I guess I will know how it feels soon enough, I thought.*

I was greeted with smiles from most of the other corporate employees but somehow not all the smiles seemed real to me. Some of the employees just looked up, nodded, and then went back to work. I saw some of the corporate cats and wagged a "hello" but they just looked at me with a staring eye, never seeming to move their head. *I thought to myself that they must be busy...or maybe they did not care to meet me.* Anyway, off we strolled passing by some of the private cubes that had doors. Bosco informed me that they were the cubes of the very important corporate employees. He called them the Corporate Coyote's or "higher-ups". I thought to myself, *"Higher up than what, a tree, or a fence?" That really confused me*. He also said they were considered the *"C-suite". I was not sure of what a "higher up" or C-suite actually was, but would remember to ask my human when I get home*. The Corporate Coyotes who had their doors open looked up at me as I passed by and said, "Welcome aboard."

"Thank you!" I said, with a great big wag of the tail. *My human said a wag of my tail would show that I was happy to be there.*

I wondered if the Corporate Coyotes ever came out of their cubes to socialize at the dog park. I would love to learn all I can and see how I can become a Corporate Coyote or live in a C-suite cube with a door. Those cubicles were much bigger with windows, extra chairs, and dog toys all around. One of the Corporate Coyotes even had a whole jar of biscuits on his desk. *I wondered if he would share.* I was getting hungry just looking at them. Nevertheless, off we went, with no offering of a biscuit, continuing to meet other corporate employees.

My tour was over and Bosco brought me to my new cube. It was a good size cube but was surrounded by walls that did not allow me see over them unless I stood on my back legs. I wondered why they were built like this. *How can you socialize if you are in a kennel with walls? I would have to ask my human about this, too.* There was a water bowl and a small package containing a few treats that was left for me, as I was the new corporate dog on the block.

There were so many different breeds and species. I have never been around so many corporate employees. I remember seeing a beautiful Collie.

Her name was Amanda. Wow was she a looker! I bet no one approached her without a perfectly groomed coat and a smart hello. I

would like to get to know her a little better!
She was in charge of education and gave classes on corporate etiquette and learning. I think I will sign up for these classes as soon as I can. *I am not sure of how much "etiquette" I have or even what it is.*

I also remember seeing a Bulldog named Charles. He was in accounting and sat right next to one of the cats. Charles was rather large and had an odor that I could not distinguish.

He was rather lumbering looking and really needed to take a bath. He was friendly though, and offered his paw when I passed by his cube. I asked him in secret if he minded sitting next to the cat and he said, "No matter, the cat does not bother with me." I asked him if the cat smelled different and he said that his nose was not up to par, so his smelling ability was not too good. He said that Oscar, the bloodhound could never sit next to the cat all day because he could smell everything around him.

I looked over the cube and saw Oscar. He had very long ears and seemed to be constantly wiping his mouth with his paw. I am not sure what Oscar did other than pawing at his computer at a constant speed.

His nose was rather large and I could see that sitting next to a cat would be very difficult for him. The corporate cats sometimes wore a lot of perfume and well, this was just too much for Oscar. *I thought about Charles and his indifference to the cats.*

We continued to round the cubes, meeting as many of the corporate employees as we could. I did spot the bird flying overhead and remembered asking Mr. Bosco what the bird's job was.

Mr. Bosco said the bird worked for one of the Corporate Coyotes. He said he was not sure of what exactly the bird did but that the bird did seem to fly over everyone's cube a few times a day. Bosco then said that the bird would fly into a C-suite cube at the end of the day and shut the door. He thought maybe his cube was located inside another cube but he was not sure. The bird's name was Daphne. She was rather pretty in color but had a huge beak! I think I will stay away from her most of the time.

Chapter 3
"My Assignment"

After we finished rounding the cubes, I settled in my chair and started to learn about my job. I would continue to think about my new friends a little later. I turned on my computer, signed in with a stamp of my paw and magic happened! My picture and a welcome message popped up and a voice said, "Good Morning Cooper, we are happy to have you aboard. Please scroll through the following screens on your new computer for your daily assignments and duties."

Now, this is high tech if you ask me and I loved every minute of it! I started to scroll through my assignments with apprehension, as this was my first day and I wanted to make a good impression.

As I scrolled through my assignments, I became a little worried, as I did not understand exactly what I was supposed to do with them. I kept reading, adjusting my glasses as I went along. I was the new corporate delivery employee but I was not sure of what I was delivering. My job description, as it was called, said I was to deliver things. The job description also said, "...and whatever else was needed by the company." I suppose I will find that out soon enough. *I can do a lot of different things.*

I sat at my cube lapping up water and chewing on my treats, reading my assignments and trying to understand the job. I did go to school but none of what I was reading was covered in school. Mr. Bosco eventually came by and asked me how it was going. I said, "Fine, but I'm not sure how to start." He said, "No worries, we will explain that to you today." He walked away.

I sat there for a least another hour just listening to sounds coming from the other corporate employees. I could hear mumbling but not really make out what they were saying due to the walls surrounding the cubes. They all seemed to be busy – some light barking, a few howls but nonetheless, busy.

Suddenly, I heard loud barking from down the hall. I stood up on my back legs to get a better view to see what was going on. It was not a strong bark but more of a "scolding bark". Either way, I could hear it loud enough. One corporate employee was shaking his paw at another corporate employee and barking. I even saw snarling of the teeth by the corporate employee that was doing most of the barking. I was a little afraid as being yelled at in front of the other corporate employees is not something I ever wish to have happen to me. *I hope that I am never scolded like that especially in front of the other corporate employees. That would be very embarrassing.* I will have to find out later what was going on but for now, back to work. *My human once told me that I should stay out of any trouble. "Stay under the radar" is what my human said to me.*

Eventually, a small and chunky looking corporate employee came over to my desk and asked me to go with her. She was a mixture, like me. (I am part German Shepard and part Shar-Pei.) If I had to guess, she was part Pug, part Beagle, I think.

She walked fast and that actually was refreshing because I had been sitting at my cube a long time. She had on a smell that was rather strong probably to keep the fleas from jumping on her. She sat me down in a room called the mailroom. In the mailroom was a picture of a mailman. There was a logo underneath the picture that read, "Mailmen are our friends." I never knew this. I always thought the mailmen were not our friends.

This must have something to do with that other word used by Bosco, *"inclusion."*

I listened to her explain how to sort all the mail for the day. She then handed me a book with all the information regarding sorting and delivering the mail. It was a large book and would take some time to read. I asked her if I could take it home and show my human. She said, "No, that would be against our policy." I wish I could take it home but I will have to read it when I take my breaks.

Her name was Ms. Spinks. She was very strict but thorough. She covered the general procedures and then asked if I had any questions. I was still trying to understand everything so I said, "Not right now, but maybe later after I get started."

Ms. Spinks also informed me that sometimes I would need to *"multi-task."*

"What does that mean?" I asked.

Ms. Spinks explained that multi-tasking was actually doing two or three things at the same time. Wow, I said to myself, multi-tasking seemed difficult. *I imagined chasing two rabbits at the same time. I don't think I would be able to catch even one if I had to try and chase two. They always run in different directions.*

Ms. Spinks handed me a phone with very large numbers on it. She said it was a "smart phone". She said I would need to keep this smart phone with me at all times. It is how people will communicate to me along with email. *Wow, I never knew that phones were smart. This will take some time to understand.* Ms. Spinks said that employees will call me on my phone if they need anything. I nodded and placed the phone on the counter in the mailroom.

Ms. Spinks left the room in a dash. I sniffed around for a while trying to get a good feel for the mailroom. I smelled many different scents, even some that I have never smelled before. *As the time passed, I wondered why so many of the corporate employees came into this mailroom if I was hired to sort and deliver the mail.* I am sure as time passes I will understand everything a bit better. I started to sort the mail by name, then by department. There were letters, boxes, small envelopes, magazines, and many other assorted items. There was a cart and a saddlebag available that I could use to deliver the mail. I decided to use the saddlebag.

Chapter 4
"The Delivery"

My day really began a few hours after I started. I loaded up my saddlebag, which was secured on my back by some rather large leather straps and started out.

"Good Morning! My name is Cooper and I have your mail for the day." I was at the desk of Amanda the Collie.

She said, "Why thank you, Cooper." I wagged my tail and gave her a big smile. Boy was she beautiful!

I asked her how long she has worked for the company and she said about 3 years. She said she came to the company as a secretary and was quickly promoted. She told me about the classes she conducts and how I could sign up. I asked Amanda about the corporate etiquette classes. She told me that they reviewed how to conduct yourself in a corporate setting. She continued to explain what the classes would teach an employee: how to write a memo or respond to an email with the utmost manners. Amanda told me that sometimes employees wrote things in emails that were not very mannerly.

I told her that I am very interested in learning all that I can. *My human always said that manners will be your saving grace.* Amanda was so nice. I will be happy to deliver her the mail every day!

I continued down the hallway until I reached a C-suite corporate employee. I gently scratched on the door only to hear, "Wait a minute!" in an unfriendly voice. I waited. I must have sat there for a whole five minutes. I scratched again only to hear, "Hold on, will you please!"

The door finally opened and a large cat approached me. She was very furry, brownish yellow in color, and had a permanent scowl on her face. I stepped back in fear as I thought she was going to scratch me. Her name was Petunia Pursy. She was a brownish mix of Persian and something else that I have never met.

I told her I was new and my name was **Cooper Schmidt**. I informed her that I was the new corporate delivery dog and that I had her mail. She meowed a bit and said, "Put it down here on my desk and in the future do not deliver my mail unless I ask for it!"

Boy was she mean. I do not think anyone must like her very much. She does not treat corporate employees very nicely. *I thought Mr. Bosco said we were supposed to get along with everyone? I wonder if she meows to everyone else like this or just me.* Regardless, I dropped her mail where she told me to and left at a quick trot. I will let Ms. Spinks know that Ms. Pursy does not want her mail delivered until she asks for it.

My next stop was another C-suite corporate employee. I scratched on another door and was greeted by a huge St. Bernard named Harry Smothers, M.B.S. (Master of Best Sniffers). A "Masters of Best Sniffers" went to even more school than a B.B.S. (Bachelor of Better Sniffers). Now, Harry was a rather large employee with bloodshot eyes and large mouth.

Harry carried something around his neck that looked like a small barrel. I asked him what it was and he said, "This is where I keep my water." "This way I don't need to get up from my desk and go to the cafeteria if I am thirsty."

Very interesting, I thought to myself. He was very nice and offered me a biscuit right away. He asked me where I went to school and offered to mentor me in the future if I so choose. *I have never had a mentor, just a human. I do have a cousin that lives with us, Lucy, but she is not very smart. I don't think Lucy could be a mentor.*

I wondered if all the corporate employees had mentors. It was grand meeting Harry Smothers and it was a pleasant surprise as compared to Petunia Pursy, the corporate cat.

My next stop was a group of cubes known as the "architects." There was quite a mix of breeds in this area. There were hounds, terriers, cats and even a show dog. I knew it was a show dog because he had a blue ribbon on his nametag. There was one employee with the title of N.W.C. or *Non-Working Class* next to his name. I began handing out the mail to each of the architects. Most of the mail was magazines and letters. However, a large box was addressed to the "non-working class" corporate employee. His name was Butch. Butch was a large Mastiff.

He barely fit in his chair, nevertheless his cube. He sat with eyes barely opened. I delivered his box and watched as he opened it. In the box was a large supply of biscuits and bones from one of the other companies we worked with. He said it was a "thank you" present. Something did not sit right with this exchange. *I wondered if anyone would send me presents such as this.* Butch did not seem to be doing much work at all but got a package of biscuits from another company. He had papers scattered all over his cube. *I am not sure I understand all of this but I have my own job to do and I will do it well.* It's my first job and I want to make a good impression.

Next to Butch sat Amy. Amy was an Afghan. She had the longest coat of fur I have ever seen!

 It was a dusky gray color. It appeared to be the kind of coat that was unmanageable. She kept a scarf tied around her hair but that did not seem to help. She gave me a very happy wag of tail, which in turn swiped all of her papers all over the floor. I quickly ran over and helped her pick up her papers and folders. Butch did not even get up off his chair. He was after all, a "non-working class" breed. She thanked me profusely and said I was quite a gentleman. That was the first compliment I got today!

I continued down the hallway, finished my first route for the morning, and thought it time for a break in the dog park.

Chapter 5
"New Friends"

I hung up my saddlebag where Ms. Spinks had suggested. Ms. Spinks said that the mail is private and no one should have access to it other than her and me. I locked the mailroom door and put the key around my collar. I decided to run down the stairs four flights instead of taking the elevator. It was good to keep in shape especially for my job. Mr. Bosco said I needed to be energetic. Once outside, I stepped up my pace to get to the corporate park. I really had to go, if you know what I mean.

Out the door, I went and crossed through the parking garage to the corporate park. I ran over to the first hydrant and well, you know what happened next. Once finished, I looked around to see who else was at the park.

I trotted by a few more hydrants, park benches, biscuit machines and grass pads. There was a couple of large trees that provided shade and easy to climb on. I spotted Charles sitting in the shade under one of the trees. I walked over to say hello and to sit with him for a bit. Charles was a very large English bulldog and he needed to have shade all of the time. He did not breathe very well through his nose and the fresh air and open space was a joy to him.

"Hi Charles," I said to him with a quick wag of my tail.

He looked up and said, "Hey Cooper, how is it going so far?"

"It's going pretty okay so far," I said. Charles was my first friend at the company. Being an older dog, I figured he knew the ropes.

I did mention to Charles about my experience with Petunia Pursy. I told Charles she was not very appreciative of me bringing her the mail on my scheduled route. Charles told me that her behavior has not been addressed by management. He said that everyone expects her to be rude, so no one really bothers with her much or helps her with anything. I told Charles that I will have to adjust my route since she only wants her mail when she calls for it. *I wondered if this will affect my scheduled trips during the day.* "What if I am busy with something else and cannot deliver her mail her mail when she wants it?" I asked Charles.

Charles said not to worry about it and to do my job the best I can under the circumstances. I said "Okay" and thanked him for his help.

Charles and I discussed a few more things before we were joined by Oscar and Butch. Even though Oscar was in accounting and Butch an architect, they have known each other for years and always hung around together. They both were happy to get out and walk a bit through the park. We only had about 15 minutes to stretch our legs, do our business, and socialize before going back in the cube. The conversation surrounded itself by talk of the other corporate employees. It seems that everyone has an opinion of the other corporate employees. *I wondered if the other corporate employees talked about Charles, Butch, and Oscar in the same way.* I thought it best to just listen for now. *My human told me that sometimes corporate employees talk about each other just to pass the time.* My human also told me that a lot of this "talk" was made up and not always nice. For now, I will just listen and take everything in, as I do not even know everyone yet. It is only my first day!

We all decided to meet and go to lunch at noon. I was so excited. I never went to a corporate lunch before and with my new friends!

After another mail-collection run, we met in the lobby and leisurely began walking toward the lunch restaurant called "The Biscuit Bar."

The Biscuit Bar was a well-known establishment according to Butch. All the corporate employees frequented The Biscuit Bar at least once a week. He said the menu was reasonable and offered such things as tuna on a biscuit, ham and bone soup or a salad of carrots and pork. I decided on the tuna on a biscuit with a side of sliced bacon. We were all served immediately with an endless supply of fresh water in our bowls. Our lunch came and we hurriedly ate, as we were pretty hungry.

Boy was I ready for a nap. There is nothing better than to eat a good meal and take a long nap. However, I had to get back to work this afternoon so napping was out of the question. Charles and I led the way back to the office as Butch and Oscar dragged behind us. We reached the elevators and went up to our cubes to complete the day's assignments.

I walked over to the mailroom with a little less energy than I started the day with. It was about 1 pm and I was ready to start the afternoon mail run. Off I went, saddlebag full of the afternoon mail deliveries.

Chapter 6
"Afternoon Run"

I began strapping on my saddlebag to finish my second route for the day. I was a little sluggish and wanted to take a quick nap but that is not the practice at this company. I lapped up some water, ate a treat, and forged ahead.

My first stop for the afternoon was the engineering department. As, I strolled down the row of cubes, I noticed that none of the employees looked up very much. They all seemed to be in their own world. I looked in my saddlebag of mail for the first address.

"Here we go", I said to myself. "Ms. Gander". I found her desk and introduced myself. Mrs. Gander was a rather large Cocker Spaniel with deep brown eyes.

At first glance, she looked very sweet and kind. She nodded at me and said, "Hello, you must be new."

I told her my name is **Cooper Schmidt** and today is my first day. She kindly offered me a chair next to her and began to talk to me about the company and the employees.

Being polite, I sat there for what seemed to be forever and listened to her go on and on about what's wrong with the company and how she cannot stand to work here. I finally said, "Why don't you find something you like somewhere else?"

She said she had been here so many years and did not want to take the time to look. She said, "I am comfortable enough." She then started to talk about her co-workers. I politely told her that I had to finish my route and I would speak with her later. *I had to get away from her as she did not seem to be a happy corporate employee. I was warned against listening to that type of corporate employee by my human.* I will have to ask Charles about her later. Ms. Gander was not like how she appeared at first glance, I thought. She looked very sweet and had a kind face but her impression of the other employees was not very good and she spoke badly about them.

I continued on to the next engineers cube. His nameplate read "Simpson". He was a Westie with an excellent blue bowtie!

He giggled at me and said, "I see Ms. Gander got your ear". *I think I knew what he meant, but checked my ears anyway.* I said, "Yes, but I left as soon as she started talking bad about other corporate employees."

Simpson said that was a good idea. He said that Ms. Gander tends to gossip and make up stories as she sees fit. "She tends to whine and well, that annoys some of the other corporate employees." I thanked him for the information and continued on my route.

I was almost finished with the first half of my afternoon run. One more break for the day in the park before my human would come to pick me up for the day.

My last stop was at another engineer's desk. I had a large envelope that looked very important. The envelope was addressed to Mr. Alexander Spotter. I laid the envelope on his desk. The envelope required his signature. It must have been very important, I thought to myself. He stamped his paw on the envelope and said "thank you."

I said, "You're welcome". He was a cat as large as I have ever seen! I asked him what breed he was and he told me he was a Maine Coon cat. He was so large that the company had to buy him an extra-large chair. His fur was gray and white and very fluffy.

I told him that I have never met a Maine Coon cat before but I was happy to meet him now. *I cannot wait to get home and tell my human who I met.*

His name was Mr. Alexander Spotter. He was very nice and invited me to hang out in the park one of these days. I said," Yes, absolutely!" Alexander had a M.B.S. after his name just like Harry Smothers and is the head of the engineering department.

I finished delivering to the engineering department and headed outside for my afternoon break. I have a lot to tell Charles and the guys!

Chapter 7
"The Scowl"

I headed down the stairs for my afternoon break. I met Charles, Oscar, and Butch under the tree. We lapped up some water, ate a few chew treats, and laid down on a nice piece of grass. *It was so nice having new friends!*

Charles said, "Here comes Alexander with Ms. Gander alongside". We all looked over at where they were going with curiosity. Alexander appeared to be snarling at Ms. Gander. Since Alexander was a large Maine Coon cat, he was almost the same size as Ms. Gander, the cocker spaniel. I told Charles of what she was saying to me while I was delivering the mail and he said, "One day, that gossiping will get her in trouble." I agreed with Charles. Gossiping is not very nice.

Ms. Gander left the park, tail tucked, ears hanging low over her shoulders. Alexander then strolled over to our group and said, "Good afternoon everyone."

We all said hello and wagged our tails, all except for Charles, the English bulldog who did not really have a tail. Butch, the Mastiff asked Alexander what was going on and why he was scowling at Ms. Gander.

Alexander said that he was discussing a private matter with her. We all thought we knew what was going on but decided not to press the matter any further. *I think Alexander was very professional by not telling us anything.*

Alexander left the park as we continued to stay for our break. Oscar, the bloodhound was drooling more than ever. He said he was not feeling very well especially being next to a large cat like Alexander.

It was a long day so far and I have met so many new corporate employees. They were all so different in breed, color, and species. Some appeared very nice and well some did not. I am sure that I will fit in and with Charles as my friend, what could go wrong?

Charles said that I should be watchful of Daphne, the bird as she is always flying around watching all the corporate employees. I told Charles that I do see her flying around but that she never really talks to me. He said that is a good thing and I should keep it that way. I asked Charles, why and he said that Daphne was a spy. "A spy, I exclaimed!"

"Yes Cooper. Daphne is one of those employees who report everything to the big corporate boss named Mr. Shearling", Charles said. "I have not yet delivered any mail to Mr. Shearling today." "I did not know that there are spies around." "Well, just do your job well and try not to speak to Daphne too much," said Charles. "I certainly will, I said." "Thanks Charles for being such a good new friend."

We continued to enjoy our break in the park until it was time to finish up for the day and head home. Oscar said that he will be in early in the morning for a special project. Butch was not worried about his project as he often says, "I just do what I can." Butch always seemed so laid back. I guess that is the demeanor of the non-working class breeds.

Chapter 8
"The Boss"

I gathered up my mail that was left over for the day. This was all the mail that could not be delivered because the employee was not at their desk or off for the day. Ms. Spinks told me only to deliver mail to employees who were present at their cubes. I had a lot of mail left over. I wondered where the rest of the employees were.

I went into the mailroom to re-file the mail when I received a call on the smart phone. I picked up the phone and said, "Mailroom, Cooper Schmidt speaking."

A deep raspy voice came on the line and said, "I did not get my mail today." I asked the employee who they were.

The employee said, "Don't you know who I am?" I said I am sorry but today was my first day and I do not know everyone yet. He told me who he was. It was Mr. Shearling, the biggest of the Corporate Coyotes.

I told Mr. Shearling, "Let me check and see if you any mail for today."

After checking thoroughly through my saddlebag and mail boxes, I did find an envelope addressed: To the CEO, Mr. Edward Shearling. I quickly grabbed the envelope and headed off to the famous cube of Mr. Shearling.

I arrived at the C-suite area and found Mr. Shearling's office. I knocked on the door and he said, "Come in."

I opened the door gently with my paw and said, "Hello, my name is Cooper Schmidt and I am the new corporate delivery dog. Today is my first day."

Mr. Shearling was a huge Komondor. He had hair that was twisted in spirals like rope. It almost looked like he was wearing a mop. He was grayish white in color with big bright brown eyes. He asked me to come into his cube and sit down.

I walked in and sat down on one of the nicest looking dog beds I had ever seen. It felt even better than it looked! His cube was larger than the others. He had a plentiful supply of biscuits and treats, even a bacon log. I was a little nervous sitting in his cube and started to pant a bit.

Mr. Shearling began talking about the company and its goals. I tried to follow what he was saying. As I was listening, I noticed Daphne sitting on a perch above his window. She listened intently and kept staring at me. It was an uncomfortable feeling. When Mr. Shearling stopped talking, he asked me if I had any questions or concerns. I told him that everything seemed to go okay for the day and that this was my first job. At that moment, Daphne fluttered her wings and squawked. Mr. Shearling told Daphne to be quiet. I asked Mr. Shearling what Daphne's job was and he said that she was his administrative assistant. I had no idea what that meant but nodded as if I did. I remembered what Charles had told me about Daphne and that she was considered a spy. *I suppose she spies for Mr. Shearling?*

I asked Mr. Shearling if there was a list of employees and their departments so I could know who everyone was and what they did. He said, "I will make sure Ms. Spinks, the floor manager gives you a copy of the organizational chart before you leave today." I thanked Mr. Shearling for the biscuits and treats before I stood up, wagged my tail, and trotted out of his office.

Wow, what an experience, meeting the big corporate boss! Unfortunately, I never met him again as he never came out of his cube. His mail was picked up by Daphne every day from that day on. Going into the job, I knew the big corporate boss was the leader. *I wonder how you can lead the corporate employees from a cube. I have so many questions!*

Chapter 9
"End of the Day"

After I left Mr. Shearling's office, I trotted down the hall knowing that I only had about one more hour until my human picked me up. Ms. Spinks was waiting for me in the mailroom.

She asked, "Cooper how was your first day on the job?"

I said, "Great!" "I met so many new people." Ms. Spinks said that Mr. Shearling had requested that she give me an organizational chart. This chart had all the names and departments of the corporate employees.

I told Ms. Spinks that I had been to accounting, architecture, education, engineering, and some of the C-suite cubes. Ms. Spinks seemed pleased with my work so far and said that she would see me in the morning. She said she was leaving early due to a vet appointment. *I hope she is ok, she seems very healthy to me. I never liked going to the vet. It almost always means a shot or clipping of something.*

Ms. Spinks said that I needed to check in with Mr. Bosco a half hour before I left for the day. I said, "Yes, ma'am." I thanked her for her help today as she dashed off. I put up my saddlebags, locked the mailroom, and headed over to see Mr. Bosco.

I knocked on Bosco's door and he muttered, "Hold on a minute". I waited outside his door for a few minutes until he came and opened it. He apologized for making me wait and asked me to come in and sit down.

I sat down and tried to relax a little. *I hope I did a good job for my first day, I thought.* Bosco started to ask me about my day. He said it was good to discuss things that went right and things that didn't. I was not sure of exactly what he wanted me to say but I began discussing my first day with him.

I began my story by telling him about Ms. Spinks and how she set me up in the mailroom. I told him about my new smart phone too. I was not sure that I should give my opinion or thoughts about a smart phone so I kept that to myself. Mr. Bosco asked if Ms. Spinks had given me the organizational chart. I said, "Yes, I have a copy." He said that the organizational chart changes without notice sometimes but he will keep me informed when he remembers. *I wondered why it changes but will wait to find out that answer.*

Mr. Bosco asked me how the process of handing out the mail went. I said it appeared pretty straightforward but that Petunia Pursy does not want her mail delivered on the schedule. I told him that Petunia Pursy wants to call me on my smart phone when she wants her mail delivered. Mr. Bosco sat back in his chair and mumbled something to himself. After a pause, he said, "Cooper, I understand". He continued to speak to the matter and said, maybe you could "reach out" to her to figure out a solution. My ears perked up and my head cocked to the side a little.

"Reach out", I said? I was very confused by this statement. "With my paw, I asked?" "Do I need to extend my paw?" What if she scratches me?

Mr. Bosco laughed a bit and said, "No, no Cooper". "Reaching out" means that you need to extend yourself by asking Mrs. Pursy if there is anything you can do to make her job easier. *Well, now I am really confused.* I confessed to Mr. Bosco that she was very rude to me and raised her voice. I explained that, she will interrupt my schedule because she wants her mail when she wants it and not before. Mr. Bosco said that sometimes the stronger employee needs to "reach out" to those who do not know how, or can't, or won't. "She is after all a corporate coyote manager."

Reluctantly, I said, "Okay, I will try." My tail sagged a bit.

We then discussed a few other topics including getting ready for an upcoming board of corporate coyote meetings. Mr. Bosco stated that I would be delivering many unusual things to the conference room and would need to coordinate the deliveries.

"Does this have something to do with multi-tasking?" I asked.

He smiled and said, "Why yes it does." *I thought to myself, this will be a challenge but maybe I can practice at home with my human.* My human can throw two balls at once in a different direction and ask me to catch a rabbit all at the same time. I laughed to myself because I think I already knew the outcome!

Mr. Bosco thanked me for a job well done for the day and that he will see me tomorrow. I stood up shook his paw and said, "Thank you for hiring me. I am excited about my new job and will do the best I can!"

I ran down the stairs to find my human waiting for me. I hopped in the backseat and collapsed.

Chapter 10
"The Ride Home"

It was great to finish my first day at work. I had so much to tell and ask my human.

We started down the road towards our home. I could not wait to lie in my bed and think about the day's activities. My human said, "So Cooper how was your first day at work. Tell me all about it!"

"Oh, it was very interesting". "I met so many different breeds and species. Did you know that they have corporate cats and a corporate bird?" I was amazed to see such *diversity*. "And they also had a picture of a mailman!" They said that meant they were *inclusive* of all types of employees." " Really," my human said. "Well, that is a good sign of an open company policy."

"Did you meet any new friends?" "Oh yes, I said." I began to tell my human about Charles and Oscar and Butch. I told my human that Charles was a massive English bulldog and that we took our breaks in the park together. I told my human that Charles has taken me under his paw and will help me as I was the newest corporate employee. I also spoke of Butch and Oscar too. I told my human that they were all in the accounting department. "We all take our breaks at the same time". "They included me since I was new". My human seemed pleased that I had already made some new friends.

Our ride home was fast as there was little traffic. I ran in the house only to see a package there with my name on it. I rushed over, wagging my tail and panting with a smile. "Is this for me", I asked? "Yes it is Cooper". "I am so proud of you!" I tore open the box and found a beautiful tie! "This is for your new job", said my human. "Thank you so much", I said. You are the best human ever!

I tried on my new tie and thought I would wear it tomorrow for my second day. It was green and black checkered and would match my coat perfectly.

We sat together on the couch where I continued to tell my human about the first day on the job. *Even Lucy, my cousin, sat down beside me to hear how my day went. Lucy was a St. Bernard just like Harry Smothers but she never went to school.*

I went through my general routine with great detail. I told my human about Ms. Spinks and how exact she was in describing things to me. I mentioned that multi-tasking was rather a confusing thing for me to understand. My human told me that many companies ask their corporate employees to *multi-task*. My human said, "That is a quick way for something to get done without 100% concentration on one thing only". "Some companies want their corporate employees to do many things at once". "This may alleviate actually hiring another employee to do a job." "It is not always easy and you don't always get the best results if corporate employees are juggling tasks". *What an explanation that was. I suppose I will try to multi-task and see how well I can do my scheduled assignment at the same time.*

I then spoke to my human about Petunia Pursy and how rude she was. My human asked me what my reaction to her was and I said that I delivered her mail and did not really say anything to her but "Okay". I told my human that I reported the behavior to my boss, Mr. Bosco. My human asked me what he said and I went through the story. "Yes, I see", said my human. "*Reaching out* is another way of asking you to be the better corporate employee and try to be understanding to those less able." *I understood that but I still did not think it was up to me to make someone else feel better.* I told my human that my boss said everyone should be able to get along with everyone else. My human nodded and took a sip of coffee. My human said, "Being able to *reach out* is to break down a barrier". "Some employees that are rude or misbehave are not capable to *reach out* and well the burden will lie on the person who is capable. " "Do you understand Cooper?" I nodded my head in agreement. "Sort of, I said." "I will try to reach out as best as I can."

"I have an organizational chart too. Mr. Shearling, the big corporate boss said I could have it. He said that will help me know who is who and where they are. He was a very large Komondor with rope for fur. I hope I see him again sometime but I don't think he comes out of his office too much."

We continued speaking for at least a half an hour and I was getting hungry for dinner and a nap.

My human said, "Let's have some dinner and rest for a while." "You can fill me in on some more thoughts of your day later."

That sounded like an excellent idea to me. I was very hungry and tired. As I finished my dinner, I curled up in my bed with my new tie and began to dream about my day. I dreamt about all the new friends I had and how much I am going to learn. I decided to write a diary each day to tell about my tales.

My human patted me on the head and said, "Have a good nap". Later we can work on that *multi-tasking* as I have a basket full of balls for you to chase!

Mr. Harry Smothers M.B.S.

Employee of the Month!

Epilogue

Lucy, my cousin, waited for me to come home every day after work. Lucy loved to hear about all the corporate employees. We sat on our dog beds for hours discussing many different topics. Lucy was always impressed with my stories.

I told Lucy that sometimes I really don't understand some things but that I try my best to find out the right way of doing things. There are so many new things to learn!

My diary is filling up with all the new words that are used around the corporate office. I can't wait to put them all together and have my human write about them in our next book!

This weekend Lucy and I are going shopping with our human to buy some new toys and lots of treats. *"So, that is what money is for, I thought to myself."*

Until next time!

p.s. Ms. Spinks came back from the vet the next day and she is having puppies! I can't wait to see them!

www.ingramcontent.com/pod-product-compliance
Lightning Source LLC
Chambersburg PA
CBHW051301170526
45165CB00004B/1810